FINAL CUT PRO
X

In EZ Steps
By
Joseph Thompson

This page was left blank intentionally

What is Final Cut Pro X

in my opinion is one of the most user friendly, professional non-linear video editing application published by Apple Inc. as part of their Pro Apps family of software program.

It is compatible with most recently released Mac computers. Operating system required to run Final Cut Pro X is macos 10.13. Unfortunately, it will not work on windows based computers. Your system should be running

OS X v10.11.4 or later
4GB of RAM (8GB recommended for 4k)
OpenCl-Capable graphics card or Intel HD Graphics 3000 or later.
256MB of VRAM (1GB recommended for 4k and 3d titles)
4.15GB of disk space.

How much is Final Cut Pro X?

Final Cut Pro released by apple sells for $300. Previously, the application cost $1000. You can buy it at any Mac App Store.

What are some of the things you can do with Final Cut Pro X?

Edit .MOV, AVI, mp4, mp4v files, combine JPEGS, JPG, PNG, TIFF
Importing files from your camera or your computer
Adding sound effects, music or voice overs to your video footage
Change color temperature of your video
Create videos for your YouTube channel
Make videos and upload them directly into your Facebook page
Create a DVD or Blu-ray Disc with chapters of your next blockbuster home movie
Modify sound from your video footage
Use Green screen footage to superimpose yourself in your favorite movie or cartoon
Add titles and text using lower thirds and other cool built in text effects to make your story come to life
Create slideshow of your families wedding pictures
Add graphics from Photoshop, word, illustrator, Coreldraw, gimp
Multicam footage can also be added and edited at rapid fire speed with powerful built-in tool
You can even create edit view closed caption text for your videos

This book will guide you on easy path on how to get started on using Final Cut Pro X to edit your video.

| 1 | Select File on the drop down menu click on New |

| 2 | Then select Project |

| 3 | Once you have a new project selected you can click on it then we are going to give it a name so we can identify our project in the interface |

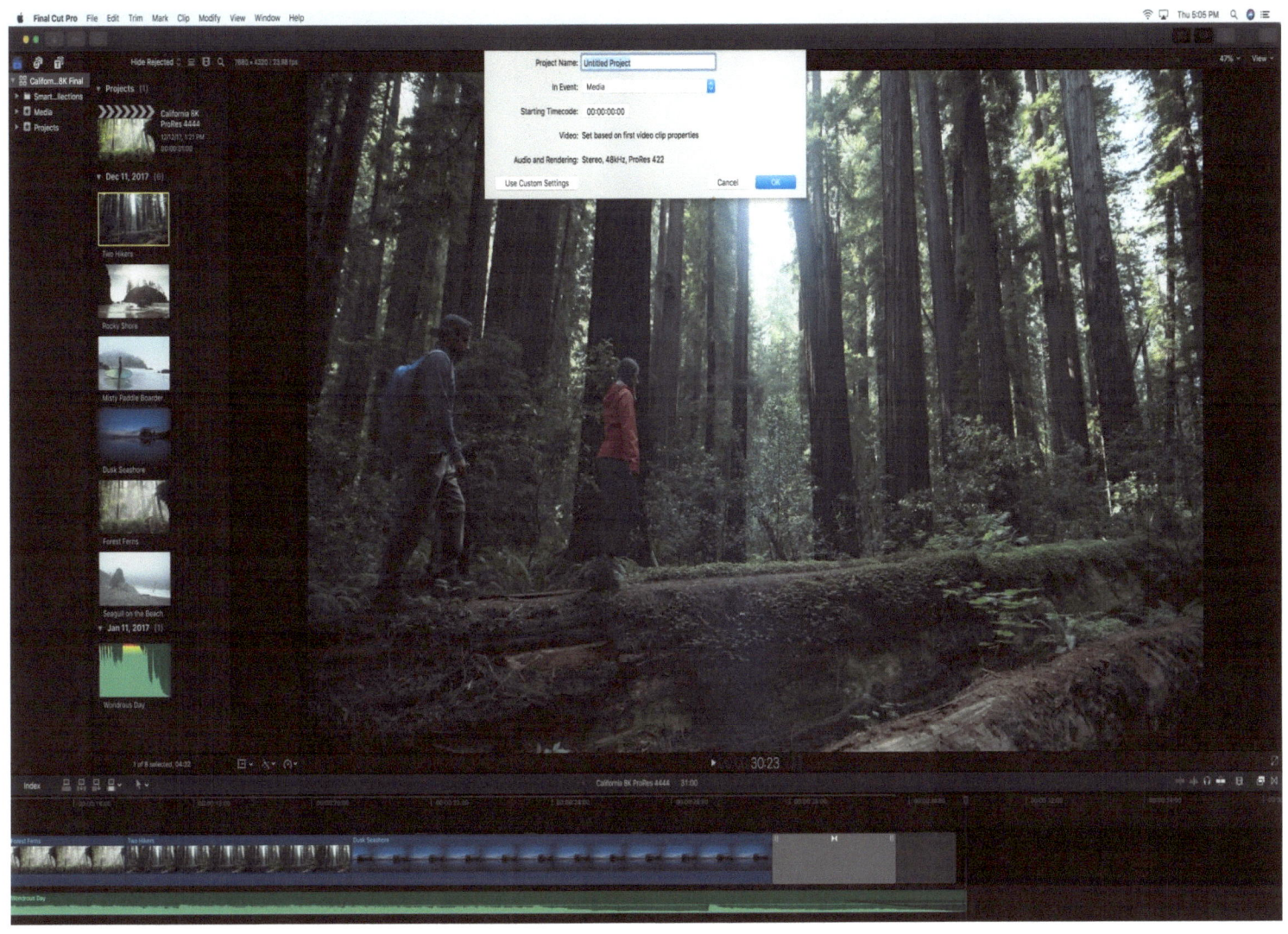

1. Once you have a new project selected you can click on it then we are going to give it a name so we can identify our project in the interface.

2. Enter a name for your project

3. Select an Event from list of choice or create an event you want to link this project to

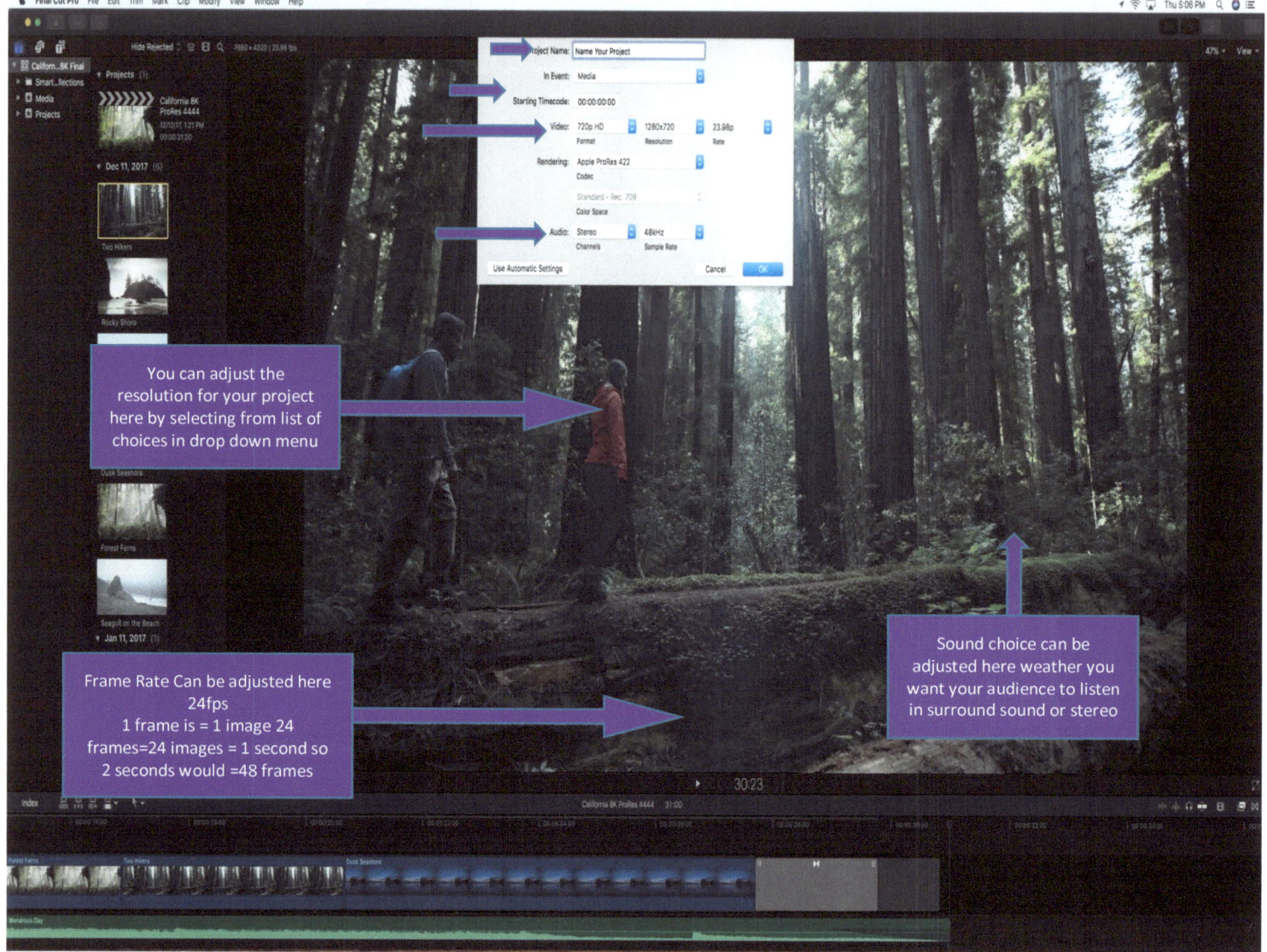

Here you can define the project setting

Timecode

Starting Timecode simply means if you want start editing from certain point in the video you can enter the time here.

Format

Video Format could be 720p HD or 1080p this comes down to a matter of preference and based on setting of your camera footage.

Resolution

The Resolution is also a matter of personal preference and original footage from your camera and its settings. Select the one that best suits your needs.

Frame rate

is different if you plan on creating a film or video to playback at regular speed select 23.98 or 24 frames per second would be ideal, but if you plan on creating a slow motion project its best to use 60 frames per second.

Audio

You have a choice or stereo or surround sound this all depends on how you recorded your sound for your footage. Did you record it using a external microphone or the internal microphone from your camera this can all have an impact on your sound quality so make your selection based on how you recorded your sound.

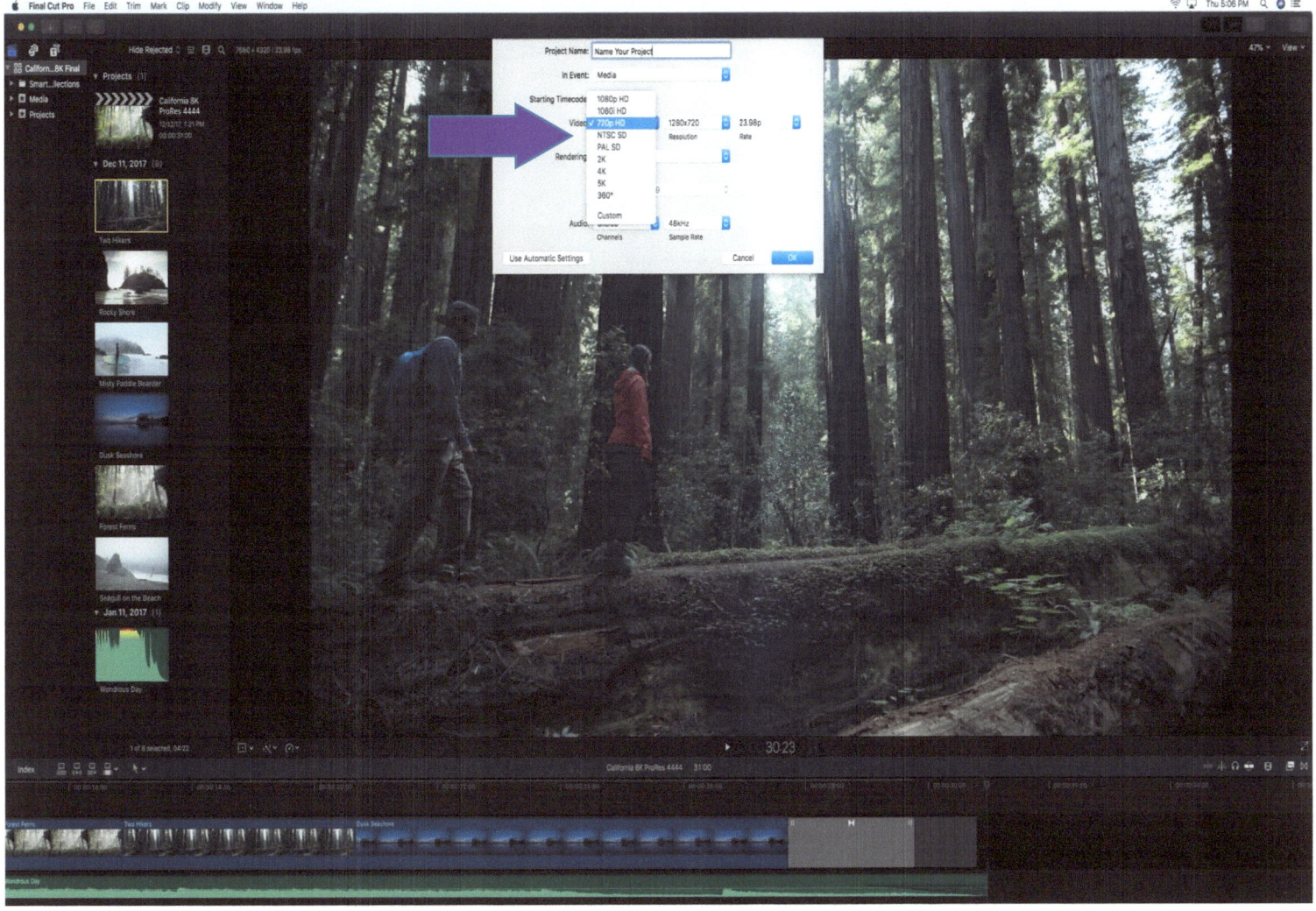

Format

Video Format could be 720p HD or 1080p this comes down to a matter of preference and based on setting of your camera footage High Definition(HD) is the new-age technology that has taken camera images to the next level. The picture is much sharper, richer and closer to what the human eyes sees as opposed to what Standard definition(SD) video camera shows you. The new HD digital cameras combined with HD technology with 24-frame progressive technology to copy a special film like picture quality in an electronic format, without the use of physical film.

Here you see in drop down under frame Final Cut Pro X comes with many choices:
1080p HD (choose this format if you are trying to create high definition video)
1080i HD (choose this format if you are trying to create high definition video)
720p HD (choose this format if you are trying to create high definition video)
NTSC SD This format is for standard definition output
PAL SD This format refers to standard definition output
2K,4K,5K and 360 which is new to this version of Final Cut Pro X

Format
Video Format could be 720p HD or 1080p this comes down to a matter of preference and based on setting of your camera footage High Definition(HD) is the new-age technology that has taken camera images to the next level. The picture is much sharper, richer and closer to what the human eyes sees as opposed to what Standard definition(SD) video camera shows you. The new HD digital cameras combined with HD technology with 24-frame progressive technology to copy a special film like picture quality in an electronic format, without the use of physical film.

Here you see in drop down under frame Final Cut Pro X comes with many choices:
1080p HD (choose this format if you are trying to create high definition video)
1080i HD (choose this format if you are trying to create high definition video)
720p HD (choose this format if you are trying to create high definition video)
NTSC SD This format is for standard definition output
PAL SD This format refers to standard definition output
2K,4K,5K and 360 which is new to this version of Final Cut Pro X

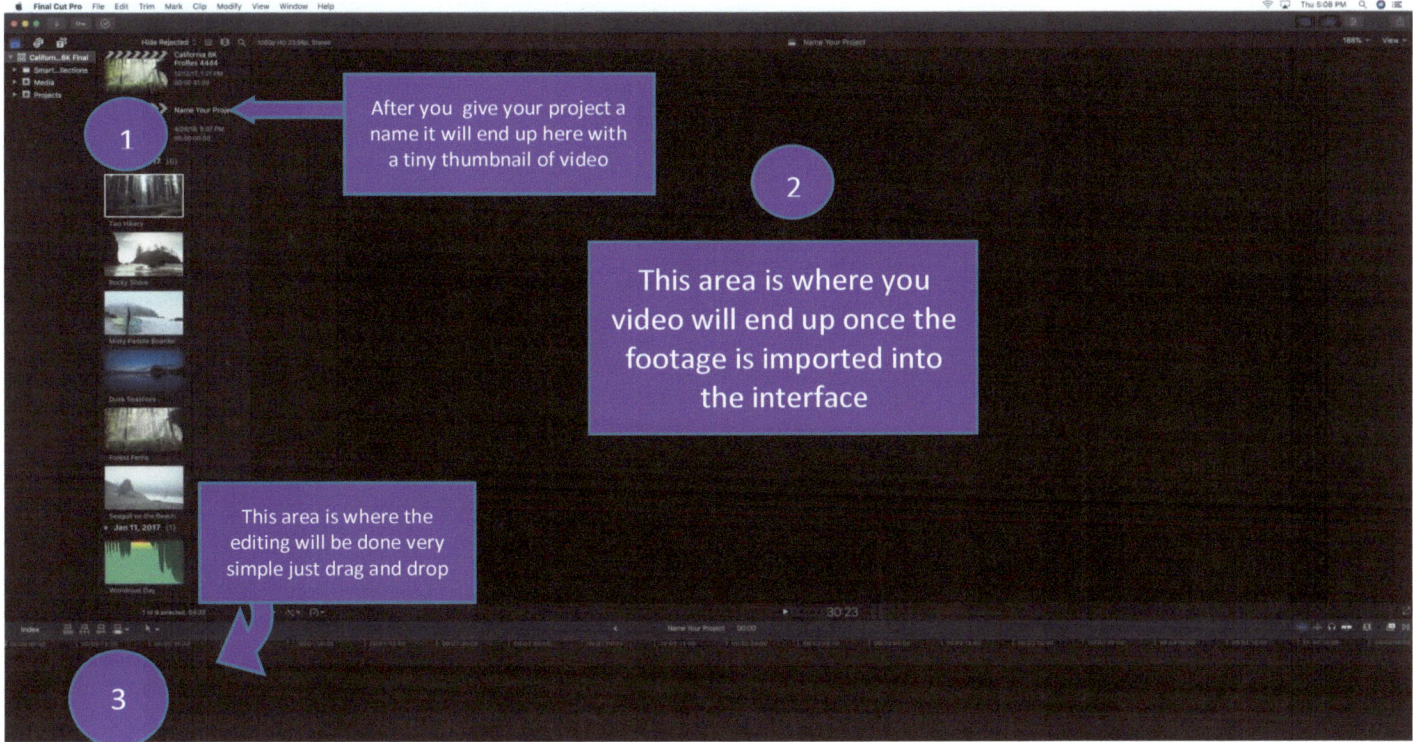

Getting Started

After you give your project a name this screen will appear empty waiting for you to now import your footage into the interface as you can see from image above

1 The first thing you will see is the name of the project on left column and any previous projects you have created until those older projects are moved to trash can they will remain in the workspace. Our project is called "Name Your Project"

2 To the left of this we see a big black empty space now this will be where you will be able to preview your work in real time as you edit. This space will display your footage time and frame rate as well as sound.

3 This area is where you can drag and drop your footage from left column into the timeline to be edited. This area works sort of like layers similar to Photoshop in you stack up your footage whatever is on top would show in area two whatever is at bottom would not show unless you use you blending mode or masking tool or keying tool and matte assuming you are familiar with what a mask is I will not expand on that in this book at this time.

1 First click on File from menu until you see drop down menu

2 Then select Import

3 You will then see menu pop out on right click on Media

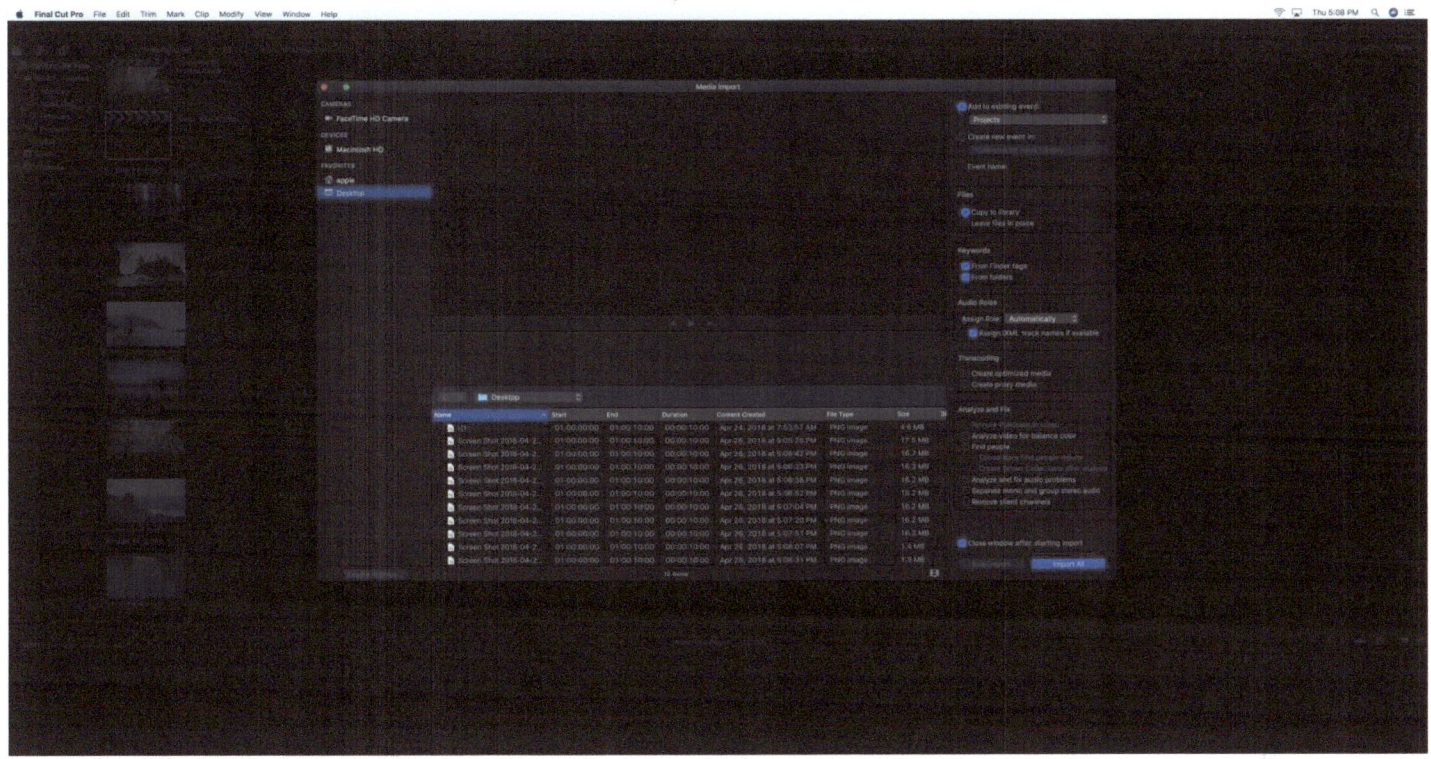

1. After you select Media this screen appears on left you will see your computer's Facetime Cam, hard drive then your desktop. I know it looks intimidating but don't worry all the interface is doing is allowing you to select the file from a location on your machine so it's accessing your internal files for import.

2. Now this area where you see all the files listed that are compatible with Final Cut Pro X displays and are all available for importation any files that are not compatible will be greyed out so this pop up allows you to select multiple items at one time or one single video file. You can also see the file type and duration of the video file before you import the item into final cuts dashboard.

3. In the right column these settings allow you to control how final cut will handle the import of the file you are going to import into the interface for example you if you wanted to copy the files to library you can select that option or if you want final cut to stabilize the footage or the audio you can select those option and it will analyze and fix it might take time depending on your systems speed.

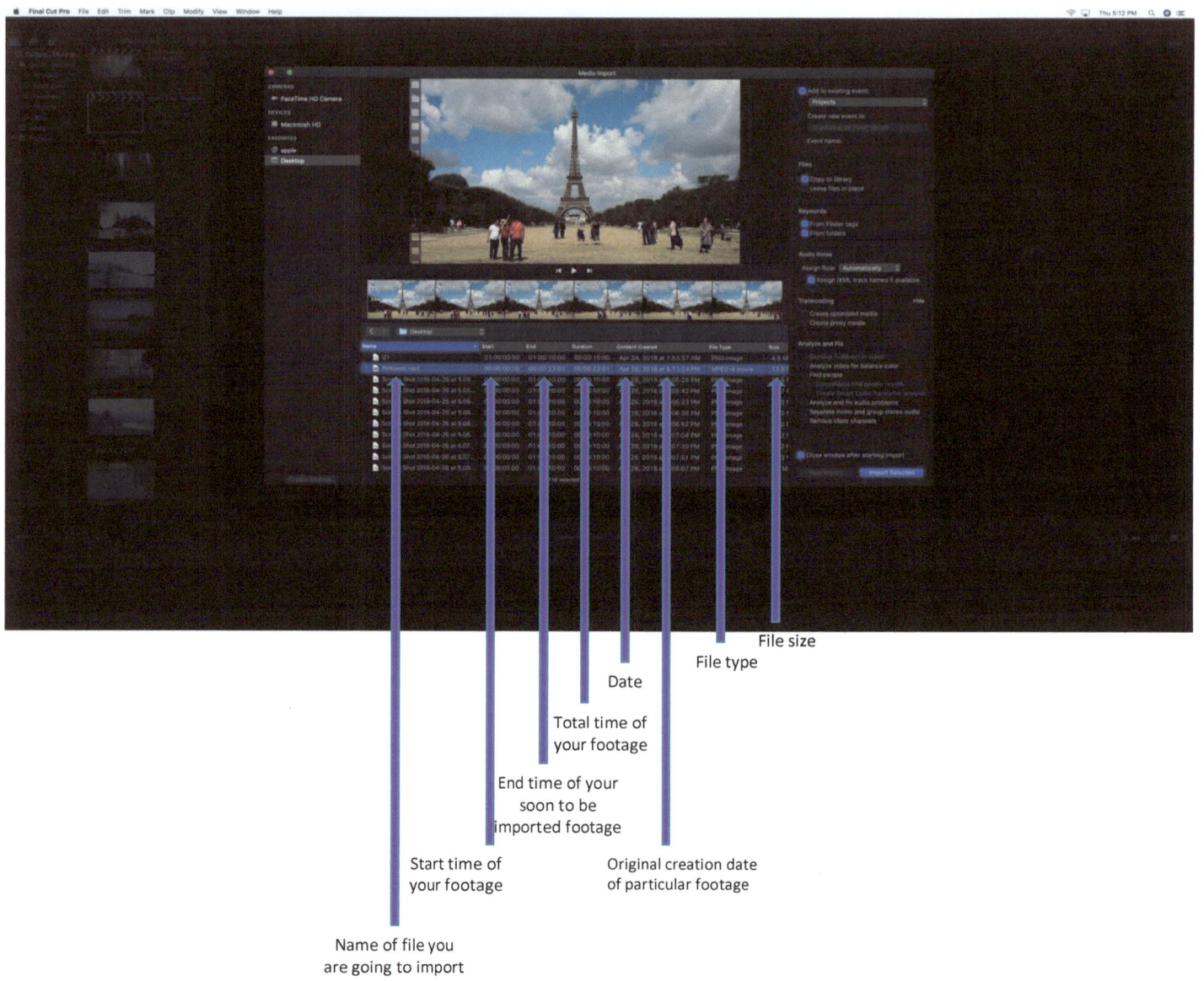

① Now you can see your video clip that will be imported into the workspace this program also allows you to browse thru the entire video so you can make sure it is the right clip that you really want to use or if you only needed a portion of the clip you can import the section you need to edit and leave the rest.

Timeline

This represents the duration of the footage that you have imported into the interface, however it is not on the timeline as yet. Taping the spacebar once will allow the video to be played back with sound.

This thumbnail is a preview of what you see on the right. This small image with yellow borders allows you to highlight and select the parts of the footage you are going to editing which is going to end up in the timeline.

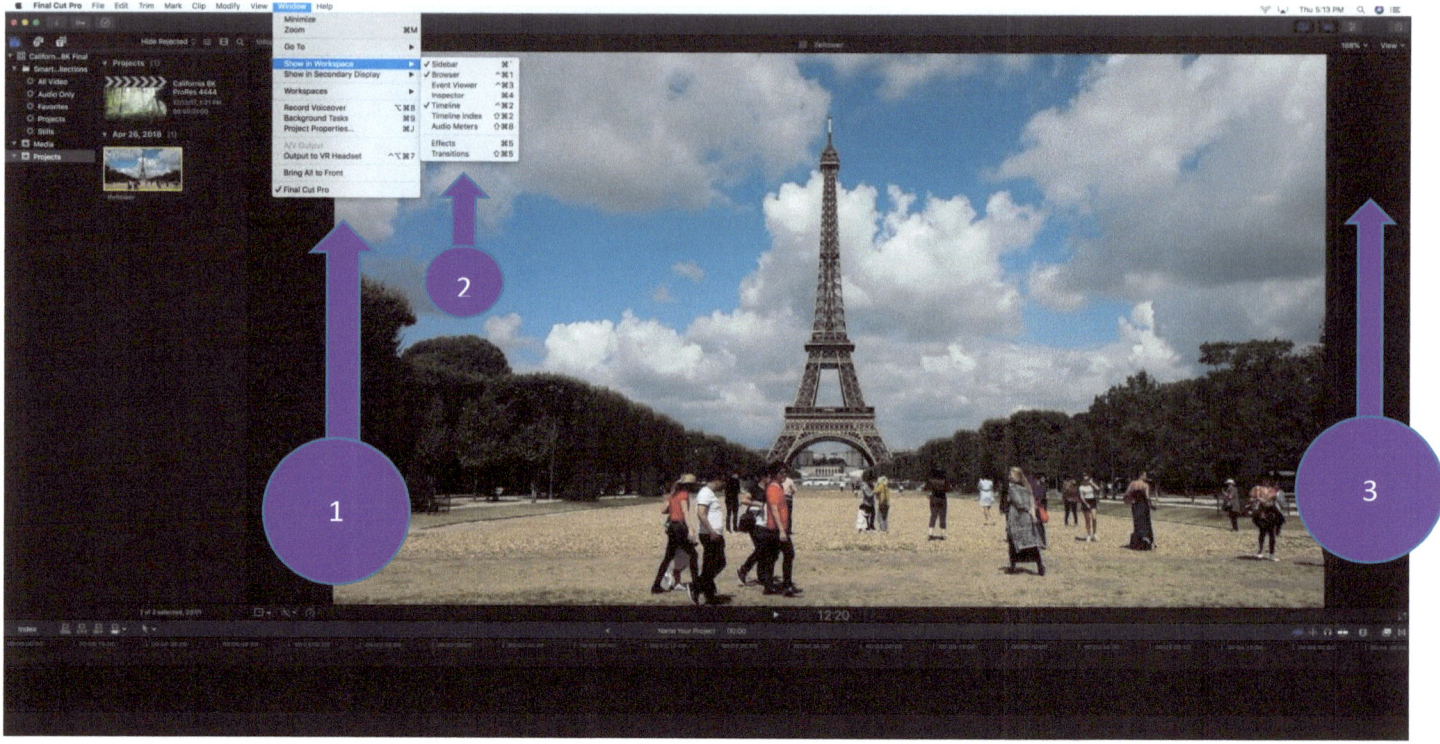

When working in Final cut pros workspace having your tool belt will help you get the most out of the program in order to see your toolbox you have to tell the program to show them in the workspace.

1. First navigate to menu bar click on Window

2. Second on drop down menu select Show in Workspace

3. Third on right pop out menu select sidebar inspector you will also see effects and transitions you have the liberty of picking the items you want to appear in the right column.

Once the sidebar has been selected to be display you should a new column appear to the right of the video the information listed in these field will summarize technical details about the video such as size, video codec and other duration of the footage you are currently being displayed in the workspace.

In order to start editing your footage you must first drag and drop, the clip into the timeline so you can begin manipulating it.
The second method you can use to bring your footage into the timeline is the fourth small icon into bottom left corner of the first column simply click it after you selected the clip you are going to work on.

Adding effects to your footage

It is not very hard to give your video clip a different look from the original footage you shot just simply drag and drop an effect and PRESTO!!! You have a new video. As you can see from the above image in right column there are plenty to choose from the only limit is your imagination and creativity. For example, you can you black & white effect if you were shooting a film about the 1800's or early 1900's to give the effect of the old days. Just simply drag and drop and you have you effect now in order to see the effects panel follow these steps to have it displayed.

1. First navigate to menu bar click on window

2. Second on drop down menu select show in workspace

3. Third on right pop out menu select Effects will appear in the right column.

17

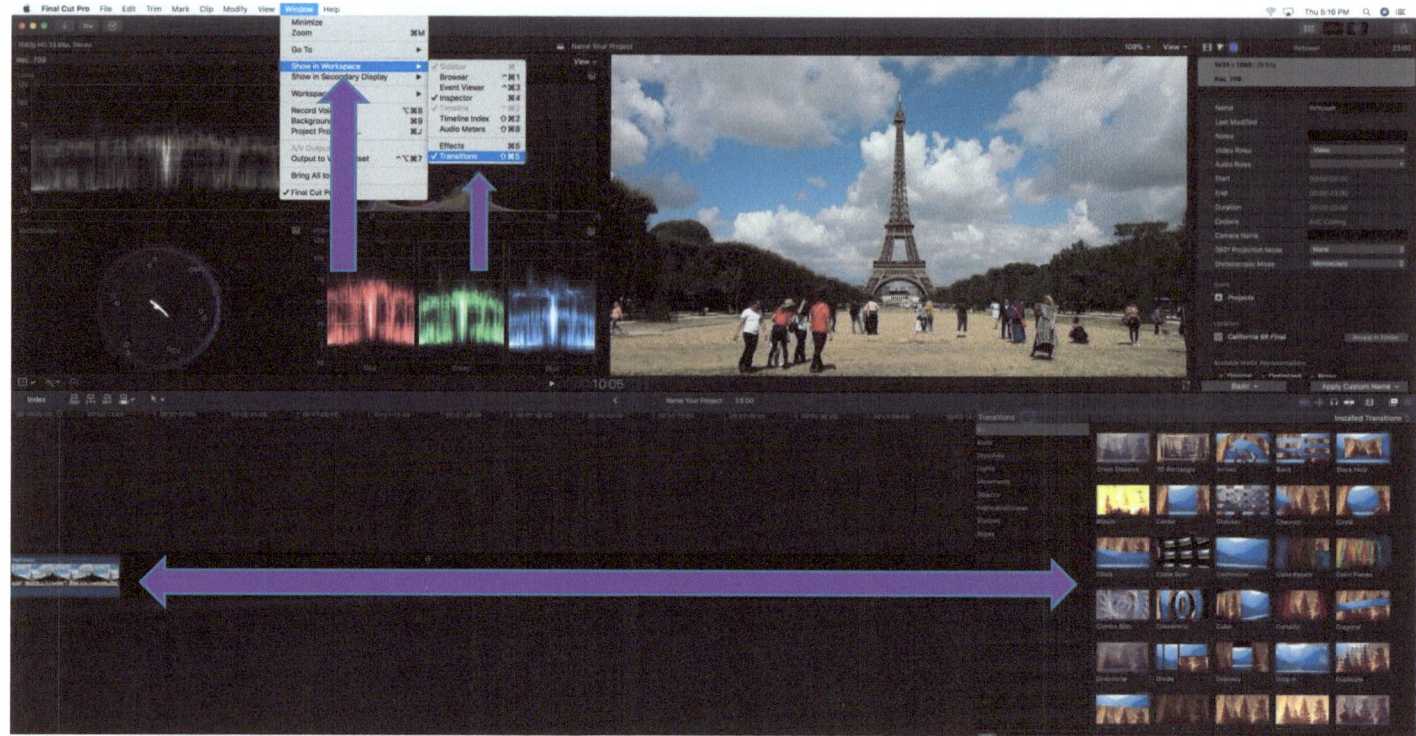

Adding transitions

Because this is non-linear editing application each clip or shot can do something different from the other clips very easy and quickly. Transitions usually are used to show time passing your change in scenery in a shot for example a family travels from country side to the city maybe you could use a cross dissolve to show a change in time of day and location. Very simple just drag and drop of your footage and it will be added you can then increase the time of the transition or decrease time.

1 First navigate to menu bar click on Window

2 Second on drop down menu select show in workspace

3 Third on right pop out menu select Transitions will appear in the right column.

Above is an example of applying a blue tint effect to the video clip as you can see the clip changed immediately. Now you can go a step further using the inspector tool by decease or increase the amount of blue tine or apply it to only a certain part of the video. You can even adjust the tint even more by using the following:

- Decrease the Opacity
- Change Blend Mode
- Increase Brightness
- Adjusting Color

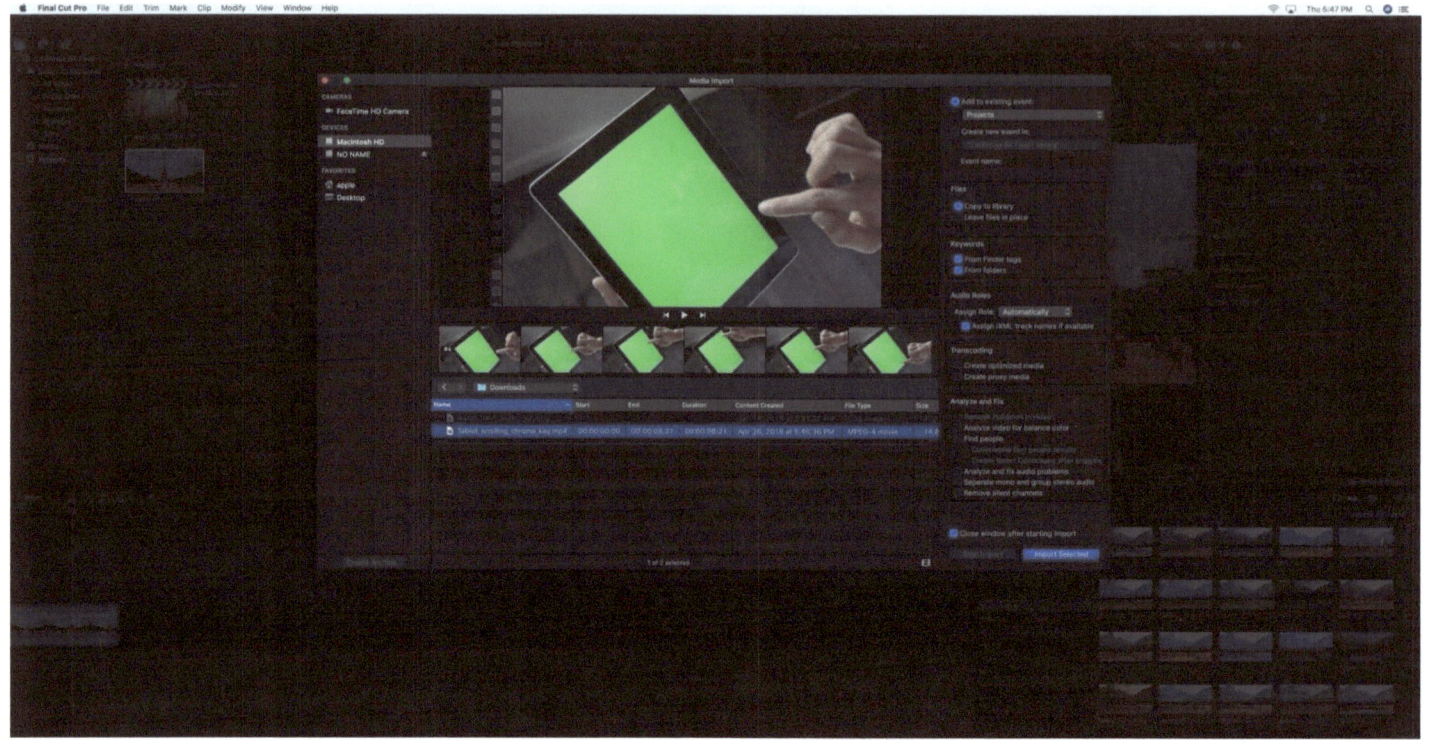

Adding more than one clip

More than likely you will have many clips here we have another clip it happens to be a greenscreen clip of a man holding a IPad. So we will how the previous clip thru this green area of the video its quiet easy now order to bring this footage in we need to import it into this workspace. Let's go!

1 First click on File from menu until you see drop down menu

2 Then select Import

3 You will then see menu pop out on right click on Media then select the and click import

Our clip is now being shown in workspace area where we can scan thru video to recheck our clips before editing it.

Now you will see our footage successfully imported into our current project. Note the title, time, date stamp and clip duration.

Our timeline now shows our green clip next to our first imported clip so in order to get it here you can drag and drop it here or click on the tiny icon.

Here you see the time has increased because we added another clip to our current footage

Drag and drop the green screen clip above clip want exposed thru the green screen

Select effects keying and then drag and drop keyer to the timeline but make sure you drop it on top the green footage.

To adjust your green screen you can use these tools to adjust the footage to get the look you are looking for.

www.ingramcontent.com/pod-product-compliance
Lightning Source LLC
Chambersburg PA
CBHW051839210526
45473CB00005B/1950